T0002106

PISCES
February 19–March 20

Crystal Astrology for Modern Life

SANDY SITRON

CONTENTS

CRYSTALS, ASTROLOGY AND YOU

UNDERSTANDING PISCES

PISCES THROUGHOUT THE YEAR

LUNAR ENERGY AND MERCURY IN MOTION

CRYSTALS,
ASTROLOGY
AND YOU

THE STONES,
THE SIGNS AND YOU

The stars above you and the stones beneath your feet are part of the fabric of your world. Astrology offers a cosmic perspective. Crystals radiate with the healing energy of the Earth. Together, they serve as guides in your life, engaged in a vibrational conversation that can help you reflect on, and tune into, who you are. Birthstones and other crystals can be used to highlight and harness the energy of your astrological birth chart.

As above, so below – harness the power of crystals and the cosmos to create a deeper connection with yourself for a confident, empowered, high-vibe life.

Astrology is the ancient study of the changing positions and alternating energy of the celestial bodies and how this relates to our lives on Earth. The unique cosmic environment that you synced up with at the moment of your first breath provides awareness of – and offers a way to interpret – your personality traits, core strengths, growth areas, emotional style and so much more. When you better understand your vibrational self, it's easier to make informed choices about the big and small things in your life. Your conscious perspective is uplifted. Your mind is opened and activated.

Crystals, or 'stones', vibrate with the breath of the Earth. They act on an energetic level, sending vibrations out into the world. They are natural amplifiers of positive energy and bring discordant energies into balance. Each crystal has its own energy blueprint, which is why different types of stones may influence the human energy field in different ways. Pairing the insight that you gain from astrology with the healing power of crystals can help you navigate certain life areas and facilitate personal transformation and spiritual growth throughout the astrological year.

Crystals and the constellations call to us. In this book you'll receive a bespoke selection of crystals to help you amplify or balance the unique energies of your sign. You'll gain insight into your life, activate your highest potential and learn to live harmoniously with the energy that surrounds you.

When gazing at the night sky, when you hold a crystal in your hand, feel inspired to slow down, be present in the moment and get ready to embark on a meaningful journey of self-discovery.

YOUR UNIQUE RECOMMENDATIONS

We all accept that different things work for different people. Advice that's a perfect fit for one person might fall flat for someone else. Regardless of where Pisces sits in your personal astrology, this book will help you understand your Pisces nature and give you specific crystal recommendations for your sign and each astrological season. You can use these bespoke Pisces crystals to build confidence, spark creativity, feel more present, harmonize relationships, attract love, embrace your emotions, cultivate friendships, create abundance, optimize your health and wellness, amplify your natural gifts and find balance.

YOUR ASTRO-CRYSTAL JOURNEY

Once you understand how the two energetic studies of crystals and astrology relate to your life, you'll be ready to take a deep dive into your Pisces energy and learn to use crystals to leverage the strengths of your Pisces gifts, whether Pisces is your Sun, Moon or Rising sign, or elsewhere in your unique astrology. You'll also discover your unique Pisces crystal recommendations for love, friendship, money, work and health to help you connect to your true potential and reach your dreams and goals.

As each astrological season holds a different kind of energy, this book will take you through the year and show you how crystals can help you channel your unique Pisces energy under each sign. In this way, you will learn to navigate through the seasons with ease and to harmonize with the cycles of nature. You will discover how crystals can help you embrace the ebb and flow of the 29-day Moon cycle, enable you to sail through Mercury Retrograde and even plan your week.

This book is part of a series that unites each of the twelve zodiac signs with recommended crystals. When you are ready to go deeper on your astro-crystal journey, you may choose to purchase the companion books in the series that correspond to the other prominent signs in your birth chart.

THE
STONES

Dazzling gemstones are typically formed deep under the Earth's surface, stimulated by the combination of mineral-rich water, heat and pressure. Subterranean 'gardens' nurture the formation of billions of atoms into highly ordered, three-dimensional repeating patterns to create unique crystals, each one holding a vibrational record of earthly, physical reality.

Across the world and over millennia, people have been fascinated by crystals. Lucent jewels have captured the imagination for over 30,000 years. In the Democratic Republic of the Congo, small tools decorated with Quartz have been found that date back to 33,000 BCE. The Ancient Sumerians of Mesopotamia (present-day Iraq) used crystals for rituals and magic in the fourth century BCE. Humankind has used crystals for decoration, status, currency, religion, healing, magic-making and, in more recent times, modern technology. Early radios used crystals as electrical and tuning components. Today's computers, LCD screens and some batteries rely on crystal technology.

Good Vibrations   People across different cultures and generations have turned to crystals as guides or helpers because it seems that, whatever facet of earthly experience you are struggling with, there is a crystal frequency that can help you move forwards on your path. Crystals may help bring calm and heal stress, empower you when you need support or confidence, or provide focus and clarity when you're struggling with an important decision. Crystals are thought to absorb the energy that you are trying to release and release the energy you are trying to absorb.

For example, if you are feeling dull and listless, Carnelian may share with you a vibration of high energy and drive. If you are overheated or stressed, Rose Quartz may help you soften and relax. Choosing the right crystal that resonates with, or reacts to, your energy can shift your mood or your mindset.

CHOOSING YOUR CRYSTALS

In Part Two of this book, you will be guided to a selection of crystals that are energetically aligned with your unique astrology. If you are adding these stones to your collection, it's important to choose responsibly.

Sustainability and Ethics   How did the crystal that you have in your hand make its way to you? The answer to this question is incredibly important to the well-being of humanity and the Earth.

The crystal industry is shrouded in mystery and plagued by bad practices. When you purchase a crystal, make sure to find gems that have a traceable, and short, journey from the mine to your hand. It's important to know if the mine that the crystal came from uses ethical, safe and sustainable practices. Discover if the lapidary, where the crystal was cut and polished, is a safe place that pays a living wage to the people who work there. The easiest way to do this is to mindfully source your crystals from sellers who have done the legwork. You vote with your financial choices. Make sure that you are contributing to better health and safety for all.

More information about sustainable and ethical practices and purveyors can be found on my website www.sandysitron.com/crystals.

Size, Finish and Price   When harnessing the power of a crystal for personal use, the size of the stone doesn't matter. If you are holding a crystal or carrying it close to your body, its vibration is in your energy field and will have an effect whatever its size.

A raw stone is a stone that is untreated. These are just as effective to use in healing practices as a crystal that has been tumbled or polished. So when you are choosing a crystal, choose one that appeals to you, no matter the size or finish.

The stones selected in this book can be sourced at an affordable price. Although some of the stones mentioned may sound ultra-luxurious and expensive, these crystals are available at a range of values.

YOUR CRYSTAL TOOLKIT

In the next section, you'll find crystal recommendations for your specific sign. First, here are a few indispensable crystals to round out your toolkit. These selections are a wonderful support for anyone at any time.

GROUNDING
AND PROTECTION

Smoky Quartz Getting grounded is the basis of spiritual work. So many factors in everyday life pull us out of ourselves. Spending too much time on your phone, not enough time in nature or eating too much sugar are common culprits, but the list goes on. If you want to nail your next meeting at work, remember where your keys are, or get on top of that to-do list, you need to get grounded. Feeling grounded also allows you to be present in your relationships and tuned in to your physical needs. This is where Smoky Quartz can help. This crystal keeps you centred, and emotionally clear. It may help you take a more practical view of a situation. On a more mystical level, Smoky Quartz has the effect of protecting you from energetic drains on your system. It is an excellent protection stone and just holding it can help you feel steady.

CLEANSING
YOUR ENERGY

Selenite Just as you bathe your body regularly, it makes sense to regularly cleanse your energy system too. Energetic cleansing can help you balance your emotions and clear your mind. Cleanse your energy after work, socializing or spending time in a crowd. Or employ Selenite to help you get rid of emotional residue after a tough conversation. Energy cleansing is also recommended when you are going through any kind of transition – a break-up, a move or some other important milestone. Use Selenite with the intention of purifying your energy field and cleansing yourself of anything that is dragging you down. Imagine that it shines a ray of light through your entire body, clearing and cleansing.

Smoky Quartz Ritual	Selenite Ritual
Perform the grounding practice on page 26 while holding Smoky Quartz to anchor you.	Selenite can also be used to cleanse the energy of your other stones. Place a Selenite stone next to your crystals overnight.

SOOTHING RELAXATION

Rose Quartz We all know what it's like to get stressed out and frazzled. Sometimes the nervous system is overloaded and it's hard to calm down. When that happens, you need a soothing crystal ally that can help you relax. If you are having trouble sleeping, are feeling on edge, or are working through some challenging emotions, it's time to soften with Rose Quartz. This dreamy pink stone is known for its inherent ability to calm and reassure. It soothes you while strengthening your capacity for empathy and compassion. If you're feeling down, lonely or heartbroken, let this crystalline stress-reliever support you.

FINDING YOUR DIRECTION

Clear Quartz Clear quartz is a true all-purpose stone. When you actively set an intention with Clear Quartz, the stone will magnify that intention. When your world is changing around you and you need to forge ahead in a new direction, Clear Quartz will get you there. Clear Quartz can help you clarify, strategize and set your aspirations for your life. Once programmed with your wishes and desires, this powerful amplifier will hold the vibration of your intentions and help you visualize and realize your future.

Rose Quartz Ritual	Clear Quartz Ritual
Infuse a tumbled Rose Quartz stone in your next cup of tea or glass of water for a mindful moment with a soothing elixir.	Write an affirmation that inspires you. Say your affirmation aloud while holding Clear Quartz.

INTUITION
AND INSIGHT

Amethyst Your intuition is your natural guidance system. It's that gut feeling you have when something feels wrong, or when something feels just right. Intuition shows up in different ways for everyone but it's like a muscle that can be strengthened. If you have questions about your life and you want to tune into the answers, Amethyst is at your service. In those moments, practice asking and listening and let this violet stone help open up your mind's eye. Amethyst is also a fantastic friend when you need help saying the right thing in your next important conversation, meeting or presentation. Or if you are looking for a sparkling boost to your creativity, open the channels of inspiration with Amethyst by your side.

	Amethyst Ritual	

The next time you have a question about your life or
path, lie down and place an Amethyst stone on your forehead or
near the crown of your head. Meditate and make space for
the answer to come through.

THE SIGNS

ASTROLOGY AND YOU

You are a unique being, made up of a solar system of characteristics that define your identity. Astrology illuminates your personality and your path. It describes how you think, learn, love, act and much more. Astrology can also be used to understand the energy of the moment.

Astrology has been contributed to by cultures throughout the world over thousands of years. The astrology used in this book is drawn from contemporary Western astrology. Like all things in the universe, the movements of the planets through the zodiac create a vibration. At the moment of your first breath, this energy is mirrored within you.

Your astrology is much more complex than just your star sign. The movements of the planets under the zodiac, in the exact place, at the exact moment you were born form your birth chart, a personalized map of the sky from your unique vantage point on Earth when you took your first breath. As well as showing you where the Sun lands in your chart, denoting your star sign, it also shows under which signs the Moon and other planets fall – this is the key to understanding your personal energetic code.

In order to discover your unique astrological make-up first you need to map your birth chart.

SUN, MOON AND RISING SIGN

When someone asks, 'What's your sign?' they are actually referring to your Sun sign, but it's worth learning your Moon and Rising signs too. These three symbols are a good place to begin your astrological journey as they represent the basic outline of who you are – like a simple sketch that captures your likeness in just a few brushstrokes. Together these three symbols make up your inner and outer self.

Casting Your Birth Chart   Go to www.sandysitron.com/crystals and enter your birth data in the 'Create Your Birth Chart' tool. You'll then receive your birth chart, also called your natal chart, that shows the signs that the planets were in when you were born, and where they were located in the sky.

SUN SIGN

- The Sun is a constant bright light, it symbolizes your ego, the part of you that you consciously identify with. It's how you tend to think of yourself.

- The Sun is the gravitational centre of the solar system, it represents your core self and describes your fundamental character and values.

- The Sun is the energy source that creates life on our planet, it signifies how you channel your energy.

MOON SIGN

- The Moon is most visible at night, it symbolizes the part of you that is hard to see – your subconscious self.

- The Moon changes shape through the lunar month. It represents your ever-changing emotions and how you respond subconsciously to your feelings.

- The Moon is a satellite that circles the Earth, it describes how you turn inwards to protect, nurture and soothe yourself.

RISING SIGN

- The Rising sign, also known as your Ascendant, is the constellation of the zodiac that was rising on the eastern horizon at the precise moment of your birth.

- The Rising sign shines new light into the world. It symbolizes how the rays of your personality beam out ahead as you walk down the street, meet new people, or interact on social media. It represents your vibe or your 'brand'. It epitomizes how other people see you.

- As you explore the following pages, you'll learn how to balance and enhance your unique energy using supportive crystals. This book will also help you find alignment and teach you how to leverage your inherent gifts.

PLANETS

SUN
☉

MOON
☽

MERCURY
☿

VENUS
♀

MARS
♂

JUPITER
♃

SATURN
♄

URANUS
♅

NEPTUNE
♆

PLUTO
♇

DEC 22–JAN 19

JAN 20–FEB 18

FEB 19–MAR 20

MAR 21–APR 19

APR 20–MAY 20

MAY 21–JUN 21

CAPRICORN

AQUARIUS

PISCES

ARIES

TAURUS

GEMINI

GARNET

AMETHYST

AQUAMARINE

JASPER

EMERALD

AGATE

DATES ARE APPROXIMATE AS THE DATES OF THE
SIGNS VARY BY ABOUT A DAY FROM YEAR TO YEAR.

ELEMENTS

FIRE

△

EARTH

▽

AIR

△

WATER

▽

MODALITY

CARDINAL

⌄̇

FIXED

⊟

MUTABLE

⌒̇

NOV 22–DEC 21

OCT 24–NOV 21

SEP 23–OCT 23

AUG 23–SEP 22

JUL 23–AUG 22

JUN 22–JUL 22

SAGITTARIUS

SCORPIO

LIBRA

VIRGO

LEO

CANCER

RUBY

TOPAZ

OPAL

SAPPHIRE

CARNELIAN

MOONSTONE

TOOLS FOR
YOUR JOURNEY

As you go forwards on your astro-crystal journey,
two key tools can help you gain insight and create positive
change – intuition and intention. Intuition helps you know
what you want and intention helps you make it happen.

LETTING YOUR
INTUITION GUIDE YOU

Everyone is intuitive, your intuition or 'inner knowing' is your built-in guidance system. Use the following prompts to strengthen your inner voice.

How to Connect
with Your Intuition

Slow down   Take a few deep breaths and close your eyes. The more you can slow down in your life (even for just five minutes) the louder your intuitive voice grows.

Pose a question   What do you want to know? Ask yourself. Say it aloud or ponder it silently. Or choose to write it down, sketch it or even dance it out. However you pose the question, make sure it is clear. If you aren't sure what to ask, try, 'what do I need to know that I don't yet know?'

Listen for the answer   You might hear words or notice a sensation in your body. You might write down your question in a notebook then flip the page and write down the answer. You might have an emotional response or feel compelled to move in a certain way. Pay attention.

Practice   The more you practice asking and listening, the more you get to understand your unique intuitive voice. Just as weightlifting tones your physical body, practicing these steps improves your intuitive muscle, so stick with it!

INTENTION
SETTING

In your meditations and rituals, you can program
your crystals with the intentions or affirmations
that will help you meet your goals.
An intention is a new thought that you would
like to think. Our subconscious minds save
energy by putting certain thoughts and habits on
repeat. This survival skill has benefits, such as
giving us more energy and space for other things,
but it also has its downsides, such as getting us
stuck in a negative pattern. One way to break in
a new way of thinking is to intentionally repeat
a new thought. Here is how to 'affirm' your new
way of thinking into being!

Define what it is you would like to change.
Where are you feeling stuck? What is the pattern
that is bugging you? For example, 'I am stuck
because I have these exciting ideas for new
projects, but I never finish what I start.'

· <u>Decide what you want</u>
For instance, 'It would be great
if I finished my projects.'

· <u>Make it an 'I' statement</u>
Such as, 'I finish projects.'

· <u>Make it affirmative</u>
Make sure your affirmation is
positively stated. Say what you want,
not what you don't want. So 'I finish
my projects' not 'I no longer leave
my projects unfinished'.

· <u>Make it in the here and now</u>
Write your affirmation in the present
tense: 'I finish my projects' rather
than 'I will finish my projects'.

· <u>Describe the feeling</u>
Include some positive descriptors,
so that you can easily visualize
how great it feels to realize your
affirmation: 'I finish my projects
and I feel so satisfied.'

· <u>Evaluate</u> Does the affirmation
you wrote give you a positive
feeling? If so, wonderful! You have
your affirmation. If not, refine it.
You may need a 'stepping stone'
to make your affirmation more
believable. For example, if you
have a complicated track record
with finishing what you begin, your
subconscious mind may need more
help believing 'I finish my projects
and I feel so satisfied'. In that case
try, 'I believe in the possibility
that I finish my projects and feel
satisfied', or 'I'm learning to finish
my projects with satisfaction and
ease'. With time and practice you'll
find that you no longer need the
stepping stone and you can update
your affirmation to 'I easily finish
my projects and I'm filled with
satisfaction!'

WAYS TO
WORK WITH
CRYSTALS

Crystals are a powerful force as they are but,
in order to optimize their benefits, discover how
to care for and recharge them with regular
cleansing, and learn how to activate them using
the intentions you've developed.

CLEANSE YOUR CRYSTALS

Everything on Earth must go through a process of decay and renewal. Cleansing your crystals can help them reset with a clear energetic frequency. When you cleanse a crystal, imagine that you are clearing it of any energy that it may have picked up from yourself, other people and the environment.

How to Cleanse Your Crystals

Make sure to research your stone to discover if the method you are considering is safe for both you and the crystal. For example, some crystals may dissolve in water or fade in sunlight. Some stones contain trace minerals that may be physically harmful when released into water.

Light: Place your crystal in sunlight or moonlight for an hour.
Salt: Immerse your crystal in salt for about five minutes.
Sound: Chant or use an instrument such as singing bowls, chimes or tuning forks.
Water: Wash your crystal under running water, from a natural water source or a tap, for a few minutes.
Visualization: Imagine crystalline light or archangels surrounding your crystal with the intention of cleansing.
Selenite: Place selenite next to your crystal and leave in place overnight.
Earth: Bury your crystal underground for about a day.

When to cleanse your crystals

It's a good idea to cleanse your crystal when you first get it and about once a month after that. Cleanse more often if you use your crystals regularly.

GROUND
YOURSELF

Before you do any kind of energy work, it's important to get grounded. When a ship puts down its anchor in a quiet harbour, it's protected from being pulled by strong waves back into the sea. As you engage in energy work with crystals, you may drift and dream far afield. It protects you to have an anchor that keeps you connected to the Earth.

How to Get
Grounded

- To begin, set yourself up in a quiet and comfortable space, either seated or lying down. Close your eyes. Imagine that your torso is like a tree trunk with roots growing down through your feet.

- Breathe comfortably and deeply as you imagine your roots flowing down through the ground and all the way to the Earth's core.

- Visualize a healing light moving up through your roots into your body. Imagine this healing light circulating through your body and carrying any tension or stress away and out, and back down into the Earth.

- Continue to imagine the energy flow – grounding energy coming up through your roots, tension and stress flowing back down to the Earth.

- When you feel relaxed and grounded, give thanks to the Earth before you open your eyes.

ACTIVATE YOUR CRYSTALS

Now that your crystal is cleansed and you are grounded, you can 'program' your crystal with the intention you've developed. Programming your crystal is one way to activate it so that its vibrations are attuned to your desires and goals. It's as simple as telling your crystal what you intend to create or achieve.

How to Program Your Intention

To amplify your crystal's power, focus your thoughts on your intention and train that energy towards your crystal.

- Make sure you have a clear intention or affirmation.

- Set a timer for ten minutes.

- Sit comfortably either in a chair or on the floor.

- Hold your crystal or place it on your body. You could also place it on the floor or on a table in front of you.

- On each inhale, repeat your intention out loud or in your mind.

- On each exhale bring your attention to your crystal.

- When you notice your attention wandering, bring your awareness back to the crystal and your breath.

- Repeat until your timer sounds.

PISCES

DATES: FEBRUARY 19–MARCH 20 ELEMENT: WATER
MODALITY: MUTABLE PLANET: NEPTUNE SYMBOL: FISH
CRYSTAL: AQUAMARINE

YOUR SIGN,
EXPLAINED

Glimmering, gossamer, compassionate Pisces. The last
sign of the zodiac, Pisces is ready to transcend the physical
plane and explore what lies beyond. As a Pisces, you find the
mystical and magical in everyday life. Through your talents,
intuition, insights, benevolence and creativity, you bring a
little slice of heaven to earth.

The Pisces motto is 'I hope'. You believe in the potential
of humankind. You are toying with the idea that there is
something to believe in that extends beyond the physical
realm that can't be seen, touched, tasted or smelled.

Being the last sign of the zodiac, there's a sense that you
hold the emotional experience of all the other signs. You can
empathize with anyone. You're a compassionate softy with a
great capacity for emotional maturity.

When you listen carefully to your heart, you receive
wonderful guidance from your intuition. You can count on
your inner wisdom because you are skilled at interpreting
the unconscious knowledge in your mind. To put it simply,
you are good at 'feeling things out'.

While other signs might formulate, limit or organize,
Pisces dissolves boundaries and the line between what's real
and imagined. By transcending the mundane existence,
you can feel closer to divine love and soul-level connection
between all people. You inspire everyone around you to
believe in magic.

PISCES IS A
WATER SIGN

The Water element symbolizes the silent language of the spirit: it's the flow of emotions, the riptide of intuition and creativity – it's everything that you feel. Sensitive and deep, you have a strong connection with your inner emotional truth. You act with care and compassion and are focused on living a life that's true to your heart.

PISCES IS A
TRANSPERSONAL SIGN

Transpersonal signs extend beyond the personal to live and work for the benefit of all people. These signs tend to consider the big picture and can factor other people's feelings and experiences into their beliefs, goals and dreams.

PISCES IS A
MUTABLE SIGN

The mutable signs adapt and shift. This energy keeps you ready to pivot, constantly refining and improving. You know how to go with the flow and make adjustments when necessary.

PISCES IS RULED BY
THE PLANET NEPTUNE

Neptune symbolizes intuition, dreams and spirituality. Named after the Roman god of the sea, Neptune steps off solid ground and swims in currents of emotion.

THE FISH ARE THE
SYMBOL FOR PISCES

The two Fish in the Pisces symbol swim in opposite directions. This represents the duality of the physical and spiritual realms. Pisces is interested in themes such as reality and fantasy, the tangible and the intangible, the body and the spirit.

AQUAMARINE IS A KEY
CRYSTAL BIRTHSTONE
FOR PISCES

This cerulean crystal supports a calm mind and reduces stress. When waves of emotions are swirling, Aquamarine can help you steady your ship and get clear about what you're feeling. It's also an excellent choice to help you communicate and express yourself.

PISCES
TRAITS

Your key traits show how you shine.
These are the special characteristics
that make you unique.

Mystical   By infusing your everyday existence with creativity and imagination, you inhabit a magical world.

Intuitive   When you know, you know. Your intuition is strong. It's as if you have extra antennae that you use to tune in to your surroundings.

Dreamy   You emanate a dreamy, ethereal, almost otherworldly quality. You love to get lost in a reverie.

Empathetic   Compassion comes to you naturally. You quickly pick up on other peoples' feelings and you have a hard time separating yourself from their emotional experience.

Talented   Capable and gifted, you have many accomplishments. This is because you're naturally good at many different things, and because you adapt and refine your techniques.

Peaceful   Your main mode is harmony. Why can't everyone just get along? Out of all the signs, you're the one who believes in peace on Earth.

Tolerant   When you are helping someone, you tend to be patient and understanding. And you're a champion for human rights.

Sweet   Gentle and kind, you're sweet like honey.

PISCES GIFTS
AND GROWTH AREAS

Your natural gifts offer both strengths and challenges. The same traits that make you special may also require balance at times.

Emotional vs Escapist You swim in an ocean of emotion. When the feelings get to be too much, you often swim away like a slippery fish. This tendency might cause you to block out your feelings, shut down or avoid taking responsibility.

Imaginative vs Impractical
With your excellent imagination and sharp mind, you create a better, more beautiful world. But when you drift away in a dreamy reverie, practicality may suffer.

Peaceful vs Passive You don't like to rock the boat and you value harmony. If that tendency stops you from standing up for yourself and others, you become resentful or begin to feel like a victim.

Sensitive vs Self-pitying You feel things deeply – an end to a relationship or disappointment at work can really get you down. If feeling sorry for yourself is holding you back, it might help to research other ways to work with frustrations and move on.

Selfless vs Self-sacrificing
Your selflessness is the natural result of your big heart. As part of your subconscious quest to save the world, you often put the needs of others before yourself. Just make sure that you're balancing that tendency with self-care. It's okay to say 'no' and set healthy boundaries with others.

Laid-back vs Lazy An easy-going type, you have a relaxed attitude. When that tendency slows you down too much, loafing around can get in the way of your goals. Make sure you have plenty of time to rest, and that you follow through when you want to take action.

Compatibility is a complex feature of astrology
because you are more than just your Sun sign.
And other people are multi-faceted too.

Friends

Tie your ship to **Taurus's** buoy. Their
soothing energy keeps you grounded.

Cancer will cuddle you close and
help you feel at home. You vibe with
the Crab's loving and soothing energy.

Tell **Scorpio** about your worries
and fears. Nothing ever shocks them.

Capricorn can turn your dreams
into a reality. Your imagination inspires
them. Each of you offers something
that the other person can benefit from.

Foes

Aries-style aggression may inspire you to
perform your favourite magic act – one
minute you're there, and then POOF! –
you've disappeared.

Leo tends to be self-absorbed, and
Pisces is usually rather selfless. The
situation quickly becomes unbalanced.

Libra needs to talk, while Pisces
would rather feel things out.

When **Aquarius** storms with erratic
energy, you'll be swimming towards a
safe harbour.

TAURUS   SCORPIO   ARIES   LIBRA

CANCER   CAPRICORN   LEO   AQUARIUS

PISCES
SUN

If you were born February 19–March 20, Pisces is your Sun
sign (check your birth chart for an exact calculation). Your
Sun sign describes your basic energy.

Just as the Sun is the centre of the solar system, your Sun
sign (also called your zodiac sign or star sign) symbolizes
the core of your being. As a Pisces Sun, you deeply value
compassion, transcendence, faith and inner harmony. You're
inspired to create peace everywhere you go. Spirituality,
creativity and love fuel you.

At times, you may need an anchor to help you feel
grounded. Finding a balance between when to work and
when to rest is important for you. And you may yearn for the
courage to face your emotions.

Because your Sun sign fuels your confidence and enlivens
your sense of self, there are two recommended crystals for
Pisces Sun. The Amplifying crystal will help you expand upon
your gifts and the Balancing crystal will help you integrate
your growth areas.

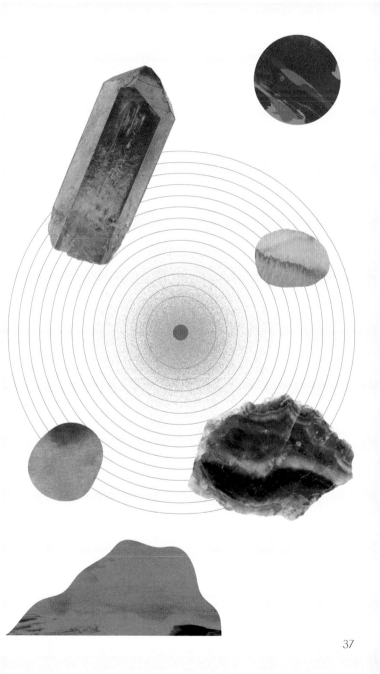

PISCES SUN AMPLIFYING CRYSTAL

COMMUNICATION, CALM, CLARITY

Aquamarine Illuminate the truth of your thoughts and feelings with the bright clarity of Aquamarine. This Beryl-family crystal ranges from translucent aqua to opaque pale blue – it recalls the ocean, the perfect match for Pisces the Fish. Aquamarine helps you amplify your natural Pisces gifts by helping you swim with your feelings and communicate clearly.

You're great with other people and their feelings. But when it comes to your own emotions, you might sometimes feel lost at the bottom of a wordless chasm, or even try to avoid the sensation of emotion entirely. That's where Aquamarine can be a great benefit to you.

This stone helps you get clarity about what you're feeling. And once you're mentally clear, it's easier to speak from the heart. Sharing and communicating your feelings helps you feel connected to others, which boosts your mood and your spirits. By opening channels of communication with the help of Aquamarine, you calm your spirit and feel incredibly vitalized.

PISCES SUN
BALANCING CRYSTAL

GROUNDING, STRENGTH,
FOLLOW-THROUGH

Bloodstone   When you need to feel anchored or you're craving an extra boost of strength, reach for Bloodstone. This Chalcedony is usually viridian green with speckles of fiery red and orange. It's a powerfully vitalizing stone that can help you get out of a slump or find fresh energy.

Pisces has a dreamy side, and you might often find yourself losing track of time or escaping your responsibilities. When Neptune's fog settles in, reach for Bloodstone to counterbalance and find your centre. This crystal can soothe and stabilize you.

Reach for Bloodstone if you feel like you are hesitating in making a decision or getting bogged down by uncertainty or challenging emotions. This crystal offers strength and determination. It can help you follow through on your goals, take action when you need to, and stand up for yourself. It helps you feel fired up with vitality and increases your sense of determination.

PISCES MOON

INTUITION, LUCIDITY, CALM

In the same way that the Moon always appears to be changing shape in the sky, the Moon in your chart symbolizes the part of you that is always changing – your emotions.

Imagine that when you have an emotion come up, the Pisces part of you steps to centre stage. This happens throughout the day. It doesn't matter if the emotion is happiness, sadness, frustration or exhilaration – when emotions arise you go into full Pisces mode. Your sensitive, intuitive, empathetic, escapist, artistic, moody, dreamy side is accentuated. You are compassionate and thoughtful towards others and you love to be creative.

You feel deeply and react with tenderness. Emotional processing is complicated by the fact that you often pick up on other people's feelings, in your empathetic way. Working with your emotions is one of your biggest learning curves.

Pisces tend to be well-practiced in various coping strategies, such as blocking the stream of emotions, escaping through distractions or closing yourself off from others. Creating healthy physical, emotional, psychological and spiritual boundaries is imperative.

Amethyst   One of your greatest gifts is your powerful connection to your inner voice. Strengthening your intuition helps you trust your decisions and feel confident in your actions. With Amethyst by your side, you can finally hear yourself think. This vibrant purple variety of Quartz helps you calm down and listen to your heart.

This crystal offers a boost of serenity and shares a quietly protective energy that acts like a balm of tranquility. With this stone of clarity, you can more easily sort out your emotions and make sense of what you're feeling. Let Amethyst help you feel strong enough to stay present and process your emotions without resorting to your famous coping strategies.

PISCES RISING

INTUITION, TRUST, COMMUNICATION

Your Rising Sign is the sign that was on the eastern horizon when you were born. It represents the face you show to the world – your social personality. As a Pisces Rising, you have a magnetic quality that is subtle and indescribable. When you enter a room, your vibe is ethereal and mystical. People are enchanted by you, and they don't always know what to make of you. You radiate wisdom and compassion.

Other people naturally tell you their secrets and come to you for comfort. That works well, because you give wonderful advice. Your communication style is loving and compassionate.

You have incredible instincts, and you can trust your gut feelings. Intuitive gifts allow you to feel out answers to many of the daily-life questions or issues that you may face. Trust yourself to make the decisions that are right for you.

You're sensitive, so sometimes it can be hard to separate your own feelings from the emotions you sense in those around you. You're learning to create boundaries between yourself

and others. Primarily introverted, it's important that you take a step back from the group and recharge your energy. Take time to retreat and reflect on your inner world.

As a Pisces Rising, you are supported by a crystal that helps you feel truly connected to those around you while forging a rewarding relationship with yourself.

Blue Lace Agate   A crystal of communication, Blue Lace Agate can remind you that first you must understand yourself. This blue-and-white-streaked silicate mineral helps you strengthen your intuition and listen to your heart. You have so much knowledge and wisdom within you. Blue Lace Agate can help you trust what you already know to be true.

Lean on Blue Lace Agate to help you feel truly seen and heard. This crystal of loving communication will help you connect in ways that are meaningful to you. Feel understood with this lovely crystal by your side.

OTHER PISCES SUPPORT CRYSTALS

The following crystals are helpful for all Pisces placements – your Sun, Moon, Rising Sign and any other Pisces planet or point you may have in your chart. Harness the potential of these stones for clarity and ease in important life areas.

Everyone has different goals for romantic love. In addition, your wishes or desires can change over time. You may wish to attract or pursue love. Perhaps you are hoping to deepen your ability to love, or to open up to intimacy physically, emotionally or spiritually. As a Pisces, you may want each love experience to take you higher and further than you've ever gone before. You want to experience everything in technicolour. There is beauty and magic in this attitude and your love really can make the world a better place. At times you may find that overblown fantasies of an ideal partnership or love experience leave you disappointed with reality. When it comes to love, you are supported by a crystal that helps you feel both inspired and grounded.

PISCES ×
LOVE

LOVE

SELF-COMPASSION

SUPPORT

Prasiolite   Prasiolite is the ultimate two-in-one for Pisces, offering a combo of otherworldly love and grounded practicality. Prasiolite can help you love yourself just a bit more. And when you feel and sense your own connection to your spirit, your heart expands ten times. This sage-green Quartz has a way of helping you come home to yourself. With your compassion for yourself at an all-time high, it's easier to let other people in. Form a solid foundation for love and open your heart with the help of Prasiolite.

Friends offer support, fun, love and new perspectives. With Pisces prominently placed in your chart, you relish your freedom and alone time. But we all need the comfort of friendship. You bring your friends the gifts of compassion, acceptance, creativity and love. Like witnessing a rainbow after a storm, you remind your friends to pause and appreciate the unexpected magic of the world. In friendship, you're supported by a crystal that can help you remember that you're connected and loved.

Agatized Coral   Agatized coral is the fossilized remains of tiny ocean animals called polyps. The polyp calicles join together, creating a coral colony that lives as one. This fossil is a wonderful support when you want to band together with your friends and feel deeply connected. A soothing crystal, it helps you create more love in your life and feel cradled by your community. It also helps you think about the bigger picture and feel filled with gratitude. Let this stone allow you to enjoy harmony as you communicate with diplomacy. Celebrate your friendships with the help of Agatized Coral.

**COMMUNITY
ACCEPTANCE
GRATITUDE**

Astrological insight can help galvanize your natural talents with your money-making potential. Your Pisces prosperity gifts are imagination, creativity, compassion and serenity. If you'd like to make more money, look to these qualities for inspiration. What feels fun? How can you take the lead? When do you feel lit up with joy and serenity? What allows you to share your kindness and compassion with others? As a Pisces, your money-management style is fluid and adaptable. It may be hard for you to grasp the details of your finances, as a sort of 'mist' seems to settle around the particulars of your bank account. Reaching out to trusted advisors for support with learning a budgeting or investing system may be helpful.

BALANCE ENTHUSIASM GOOD HABITS

Ametrine   Ametrine is a combination of Amethyst and Citrine, both silicate crystals. This purple-and-sienna-coloured stone radiates with a balance of serenity and enthusiasm. When you want to feel serene and go with the flow financially, Ametrine is there for you. When you yearn for action and motivation, Ametrine has also got you covered. This glittery gem can help you find balance if you are either too worried about money or too vague about it. Reach for this crystal when you need to establish good habits, like balancing your books or focusing on your budget. If you are looking for fresh income streams, this encouraging crystal can help you get fired up and try new things.

PISCES x
WORK

Your work must make your heart sing, Pisces! You put your all into what you do. Boundaries are not your strong suit. You may follow a career path because it makes you feel as if you are 'transcending reality', such as an art form, or a religious or spiritual calling. Or you may yearn to help the world through healing and compassionate work. Other Pisces choose a vocation for the stability it offers, which may otherwise be hard to create with your dreamy temperament. Create lots of time for unfocused activity in your calendar. This time can also help you clear your mind so that you can move through mental fog and make decisions. You are multi-talented, and you can become excellent at almost anything, as long as your heart is in it.

Green Fluorite Green Fluorite energizes you and helps you keep moving forwards. This minty-green crystal gives you a nice boost so that you can take risks, have fun and make clear decisions at work. The clarity that Green Fluorite offers helps you in your everyday work life. And it helps you make good choices when you are in times of transition. Powerful Green Fluorite can serve as your inspiration to set healthy limits so that you feel energized and have a chance to enjoy your work life. It can help you set boundaries like protecting your days off, or creating expectations around tasks or communication.

LUCIDITY
DECISIVENESS
BOUNDARIES

Much of your health and well-being comes down to how you are feeling emotionally. Make sure to reach out for assistance when you need it, as you thrive when you feel supported by, and connected to, others. You can quickly forget about the basic needs of your body, so make sure you get plenty of rest and drink lots of water. You get a lot of joy from letting yourself exist outside of a timeframe. Time spent alone or in retreat is often very healing for you. It's important for you to be very kind to yourself and make efforts to boost yourself up emotionally. Caring for a pet or spending time in nature (particularly near water) are big stress-relievers for you. Reach for a supportive crystal that helps you ease your mind and expands your sense of joyfulness.

VITALITY
JOY
SUPPORT

Purple Opal Erase anything that is stressing you out with the joy and enthusiasm offered by Purple Opal. With its upbeat energy it may offer a generous boost for your health and well-being. Purple Opal has a milky-white colour, streaked with deep purple. This comforting stone may remind you to reach out to others and share your true feelings. Its soothing energy helps you feel that support is all around you and you don't have to go it alone. Enjoy the energy of this lively and soothing stone as it helps you feel vitalized and connected.

PISCES
THROUGHOUT
THE YEAR

The energies of the zodiac signs affect us throughout the year. In astrology, there is a season for everything. Feeling separated from nature's cycles and rhythms can make you feel out of step or off-kilter. It may add to stress and drain energy. Understanding and attuning to astrology's seasons might help you feel enlivened.

Take this attunement one step further by using crystals to amplify the unique energy of each moment, so that you feel fully aligned with the rhythms of nature.

The following pages take you on a journey with the sun as it passes through the twelve signs of the zodiac on its annual rotation. You will discover the key energies of each season, along with a sign-specific horoscope that aligns with the important themes of your unique chart.

CONFIDENCE AND LEADERSHIP

Aries season is the signal that begins the horse race. And they're off! This is the moment to gallop at top speed towards your goals. Put yourself out there with confidence. Make bold decisions and step in time with your intuition. This season is about saying YES to who you are and living your life with freedom. The buds are beginning to emerge and new life is beginning. Sync up with this feeling of potential and possibility.

PISCES HOROSCOPE FOR ARIES SEASON

With the Sun moving through your zone of safety, security, money and self-worth, your attention is drawn to practical matters. Discover what helps you feel stable and resilient. Maybe your sense of security arises from a deep trust in yourself, or maybe it soothes you to have money in the bank. Slow down and make a realistic assessment.

Affirmation

I AM ENOUGH AND I AM READY.

Morning Practice	**Evening Practice**
Get your heart rate up with some fiery cardio exercise.	Cool down that inner fire with a soothing herbal tea.

CRYSTALS FOR ARIES SEASON

CONFIDENCE

Hessonite Garnet   Developing confidence is a practice of establishing deep self-trust. Let Hessonite Garnet's activating and powerful energy help you build up your courage so that you can just go for it. Also try Green Aventurine, Orange Calcite or Malachite.

LIVING BOLDLY

Pink Aventurine   When the time is ripe for taking bold action, Pink Aventurine can help you advance into your next adventure. Reach for it when you need a boost of fun. This spirited crystal connects you with your heart centre, and acts as your best accomplice in bravery and boldness. Or choose Ruby, Tangerine Quartz or Sardonyx.

DRIVE

Fire Agate   Aries season is the vehicle in which to follow your passions and desires, which makes Fire Agate the gasoline. Whether you need to get an important project going or just tackle spring cleaning, put yourself on track to get things done by syncing up with the vibration of this fierce crystal. You could also reach for Bloodstone, Stromatolite or Cinabrite.

MONEY AND
SELF-WORTH

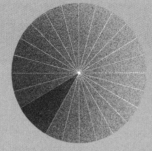

Like working in a garden and then enjoying the beauty that you've cultivated, Taurus represents sustained effort that leads to a productive reward. This season is the prime time to focus on building up your sense of personal worth and value. On one level, this process may involve nurturing your self-esteem. On another level, this may include thinking about security, money and finances. Taurus season is also a time to remember the beauty of life. It reminds us that no matter what is going on, there are simple pleasures to be had.

PISCES HOROSCOPE
FOR TAURUS SEASON

This is a mentally stimulating season for you, Pisces, as the Sun is moving through your sector of learning and socializing. Your mind may feel lit up with wonder and curiosity. Or you may feel like mixing and mingling with friends, both new and old. Light up your mind with fresh ideas and expand your social circles.

Morning Practice

Practice gratitude by reminding yourself of three things you're grateful for.

Evening Practice

Do something that feels good to your body, like stretching or wearing soft clothing.

CRYSTALS FOR TAURUS SEASON

MONEY MAGIC

Green Jade   No matter where you are beginning financially, Green Jade will juice up your money situation. This abundance stone has a way of amplifying your potential. A soft and expansive prosperity stone that soothes the spirit, it will support you as you make wise financial decisions. Reach for it when you crave a feeling of security. You could also use Pyrite, Emerald or Epidote.

SELF-WORTH

Red Jasper   Red Jasper will amp up your self-appreciation quotient. Choose Red Jasper when you're feeling uncertain, if your confidence could use a boost, or if you want to feel more resilient in any way. This stone will get you in the groove of trusting your own value. Also try Carnelian, Chrysocolla or Bixbite.

ABUNDANCE

Green Apatite   If you are feeling like something in your life is lacking, such as money, time, energy, sleep, or support, for example, you might need to boost your sense of abundance. Taurus season is the perfect time to grasp hold of that feeling of nature's plentifulness. Use Green Apatite to replenish your energy and help you feel satisfied and satiated with what you have. You could also reach for Golden Tourmaline, Uvarovite Garnet or Agate.

VALUES
AND COMMUNITY

Gemini energy is like a buzzing bee that moves from flower to flower in a garden. This season is a time of mental stimulation, new ideas, learning, communicating and sharing. Use Gemini season to evaluate or challenge your mindset and values. Which attitudes are no longer serving you? What's truly important to you? Gemini season is also a time to connect with others in the community. What can you learn from others? What can you teach others? It's a fun and lively season full of new connections.

PISCES HOROSCOPE
FOR GEMINI SEASON

Gemini season holds an extraverted energy for most people, but Pisces may feel called to spend more time at home. This time could be spent either in quiet meditation or with those special people in your innermost circle. Let your emotions flow, and be gentle with yourself. Make sure your home zone feels cosy and comfortable.

Morning Practice	Evening Practice
Help a new mindset emerge with a potent Gemini season intention.	Before falling asleep, envision yourself having a great time at a party surrounded by everyone you love.

CRYSTALS FOR GEMINI SEASON

MASTER YOUR MINDSET

Heliodor   Have repeating thoughts, fears or anxieties been plaguing you? Use the revitalizing energy of Gemini season and Heliodor to hit the reset button on these old thought patterns. This stone will gently help you harmonize your thoughts and adjust your mindset, helping you reconnect with your true values. Alternatively, try Blue Lace Agate, Chrome Chalcedony or Dragonstone.

CONNECTING

Agatized Coral   When you really want to feel connected, seen, heard and understood, reach for Agatized Coral. This fossilized coral nudges you to reach out to others and helps you analyse your relationships, whether with friends, lovers, family, neighbours or colleagues. It relays an upbeat feeling so that you can view your relationships with the people in your life with optimism. You may also choose Citrine, Apricot Agate or Bismuth.

COMMUNICATION

Aquamarine   Aquamarine is your crystal-clear communication companion. Communication helps us feel connected, and allows us to learn and grow. In those moments when you feel confused or foggy, this elegant stone will help you become grounded and steady. Use Aquamarine to find your voice – it will help you tune into your own true message and the truth of those around you. Alternatively, reach for Turquoise, Prairie Tanzanite or Green Chrysocolla.

HOME AND NURTURE

Come on home to Cancer season. Like Cancer's symbol, the Crab, wrap yourself in a protective shell and reflect on your life and your feelings. In Cancer season, engage in meaningful self-care, and also put your energy into nurturing others. Discover what makes you feel safe and cosy. This could be your actual home, your closest relationships or tending to the feelings and needs of your inner child.

PISCES HOROSCOPE FOR CANCER SEASON

Feel young at heart, creative and free! The Sun is touring your zone of individuality and self-expression. What do you simply love to do? When do you feel lit up with joy and energy? How can you express your true self to the world? The answers to these questions may reinvigorate your spirit.

Morning Practice

Let your inner child take the lead: what do they want to do today?

Evening Practice

Sing a lullaby to soothe your inner child before bed.

CRYSTALS FOR CANCER SEASON

NURTURING

Blue Calcite   What do you want to actively care for? Yourself? A child? A creative project? In order to feel truly nurturing, you need to feel inspired by love. Blue Calcite will help you soften and open up your heart centre, so that you feel drawn to put your compassionate and attentive energy where it is needed most. Other nurturing crystals include Moonstone, Blue Chalcedony and Bumblebee Jasper.

HOME ENVIRONMENT

Pink Mangano Calcite   Home is where you are safe and protected. It's your emotional nest where you can relax. Use Pink Mangano Calcite to create a grounded and peaceful home environment. This stone acts as a balm that will help you feel harmonized. Place this rosy crystal in your inner sanctum and set the intention to soothe conflict and soften your environment so that you can restore your energy after a long day or week. You could also try Chiastolite, Rose Quartz or Peach Moonstone.

FAMILY BONDS

Bornite   Family, whether chosen or blood-related, represent some of our closest relationships. Use Bornite to foster the strength of family relationships. This is a joyful stone that will help you embrace the positives that come from your family circle, while at the same time grounding you to help you remember who you are as an individual. Also try Orange Calcite, Indigo Gabbro or Girasol Quartz.

CREATIVITY AND FUN

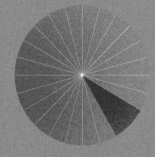

Harnessing your creativity and expressing your true self with others, that's the key to making the most of Leo season. It's all about playful sharing and creative shining. Radiate your magnificent heart of gold outwards with immediacy, freedom, spontaneity, generosity and a giant sense of fun. During this season of wholehearted self-expression, take a little time to remember how unique you are. Remember what inspires you and reflect on what you love most about yourself.

PISCES HOROSCOPE FOR LEO SEASON

Now it's time to get back to basics. With the Sun shining a spotlight on themes of organization, time-management, health and work, you may feel inspired to revamp your routines. You may have more energy for the details of life, even the more mundane aspects. Use this season's energy as an inspiration to get yourself set up for success.

Morning Practice	Evening Practice
Create daily.	Seek out a chance to laugh every day and go to bed with a smile on your face.

CRYSTALS FOR LEO SEASON

INSPIRATION

Rutilated Quartz   Inspiration is the creative spark and Rutilated Quartz can help you turn that spark into a roaring bonfire. Make Leo season feel lit up with creativity. Keep Rutilated Quartz by your side when you need an inventive solution to a problem at work, when your love life could use an inspiring reboot, or when you are ready to awaken the artist within. Set your intentions and let this highly programmable stone carry the flame of your dreams. You could also use Sunstone, Golden Labradorite or Yellow Sapphire.

SELF-APPRECIATION

Thulite   Leo season is the time to shed all insecurities and put your faith in your one true self. Loving yourself dissolves insecurity and self-criticism. Thulite tunes you into the vibration of love, peace and harmony, allowing you to be present and wholly yourself. Alternatively, reach for Ruby, Larimar, or Desert Jasper.

COURAGE

Golden Apatite   To ensure your lion-heartedness knows no bounds, you need to fire up your courage. Golden Apatite bestows upon you both passion and discernment, which determine which fears are baseless. Use it when you need to take a risk at work, strike up a conversation with someone you admire or stand up for your values. Other courage-giving crystals are Carnelian, Iolite-Sunstone or Citrine.

HEALTH
AND HABITS

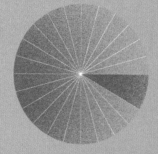

Our goals and dreams require a big-picture view,
but Virgo season reminds us that life is actually lived in the
small details. Focus on how you are living your life, your
everyday routines and rituals. On a practical level, what is
important to you? Virgo energy helps you take a closer
look at your health and habits, and how you can be
of service to others as well.

PISCES HOROSCOPE
FOR VIRGO SEASON

Relationships demand your attention.
Get clear about what you need
and want in those important one-
on-one partnerships. The Sun is
moving through your area of balance
and compromise. It's all about
communication, and creating an
understanding between two people.
Express yourself with wisdom,
compassion and clarity.

Morning Practice	**Evening Practice**
Drink a glass of water first thing.	Write down one task you're going to complete tomorrow, and stick to it.

CRYSTALS FOR
VIRGO SEASON

FOCUS

Clear Quartz   Virgo season ushers in a chance to notice the details and get focused. Use Clear Quartz to take you all the way there. This cleansing stone helps you rivet your attention on your commitments. When you program Clear Quartz with your intention for focus, you'll find that it supports you, whether you have a tight deadline or you just really need to concentrate. You could also turn to Vanadinite, Amazonite or Tiger Iron.

HEALTH

Chevron Amethyst   A lot of factors go into maintaining optimum health: genetics, diet, exercise, access to care, to name just a few. Virgo season energy will encourage you to think wisely about the preventative measures that you can take to boost both your mental well-being and physical health. Use Chevron Amethyst for gentle motivation that can help you happily embrace healthier choices. Or try Girasol Quartz, Ruby Fuchsite or Black Tourmaline.

ALTRUISM

Stromatolite   Humanity wouldn't be a successful species without the desire to be of service to others. Virgo season plus Stromatolite is your recommendation for kindness and selfless action. Turn your attention to what you can do to help others, whether that's volunteering, making a donation to a good cause, or simply smiling and being friendly. Let Stromatolite amplify your altruistic nature. Alternatively, reach for Stichtite, Rhodonite or Rose Quartz.

RELATIONSHIPS
AND BALANCE

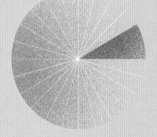

Libra season is symbolized by balanced scales.
It's a chance to look at all life areas and judge the
equilibrium. Are your relationships in balance? Do both
people in your relationships have what they want and
need? This can be a fun and harmonious time to socialize.
During Libra season, balance can also be created in your
environment through art, decoration and organization.
The scales are the symbol for justice and Libra season brings
a collective yearning to make the systems of government
more fair and to expose inequalities.

PISCES HOROSCOPE
FOR LIBRA SEASON

Just as the leaves fall from the trees in the autumn, there is always a season to let go and make way for new growth. Letting go and releasing can be emotional, and this is an important time to feel all of your feelings. Be very gentle with yourself. The Sun is currently lighting up the theme of transformation, so trust that, as you release the past, you are preparing for the future.

BALANCE EXISTS IN ALL AREAS OF MY LIFE.

Morning Practice

Reach out and message someone who is important to you, and tell them why.

Evening Practice

Meditate to create mental balance.

CRYSTALS FOR
LIBRA SEASON

HEALTHY BOUNDARIES

Iolite   Communicating what you want, need and desire is a great starting point to gain clarity in your relationships. Iolite can help you reflect and get to know yourself – the first step to speaking and sharing your truth with others. Once your inner base is stabilized, Iolite can help you reach out to another person, while maintaining your own healthy boundaries. This healing stone has a peaceful energy that helps you create balance between yourself and a partner. You could also use Amazonite, Purple Jade or Chiastolite.

BALANCE

Shungite   Balance is an active state, requiring constant adjustment. It comes under the jurisdiction of the intellectual, analytical sign of Libra. Keep checking in with yourself throughout Libra season to determine what needs more balance. For a crystal that will help you stay steady, reach for Shungite. Or choose Diopside, Selenite or Turquoise.

DECISIVENESS

Ametrine   Libra season is an excellent time to analyse, think things through and come up with new ideas. Keep Ametrine by your desk for productive planning sessions and for when you have big decisions to make. This balancing stone will help you keep your life on track. As an alternative, try Variscite, Fluorite or White Sapphire.

TRANSFORMATION AND FORGIVENESS

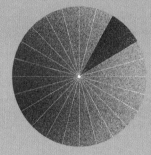

Scorpio season pulls you deeper – emotionally, physically and spiritually. This is a season of transformation, helping you to feel deeply, release old emotions and thought patterns, and get ready to move on to the next stage. By pulling back the layers and being honest with the truth of who you are, it's also an opportunity to deepen your relationships with others by letting them get to know the real you.

PISCES HOROSCOPE FOR SCORPIO SEASON

Break free from your limitations and broaden your horizons. This is an excellent time to travel and explore. You can travel physically or mentally, but either way, get inspired by a fresh perspective. As you encounter new ways of thinking, you may find that your values and philosophies about life are reinvigorated.

Morning Practice	Evening Practice
Forgive yourself for something.	Forgive someone else for something.

CRYSTALS FOR SCORPIO SEASON

INTIMACY

Red Tourmaline   Scorpio season propels you to create warmth and closeness. But opening yourself up to the vulnerability of intimacy demands courage. Whether you are setting the stage for sexual intimacy or emotional intimacy, Red Tourmaline will help you feel confident enough to embrace deep connection with others. Other crystals for intimacy are Garnet, Shiva Lingam or Red Aventurine.

TRANSFORMATION

Moldavite   Transformation brings both endings and new beginnings. Moldavite will help you spiritually and emotionally adjust when change comes into your life – when a relationship has run its course, a shift is needed in the work arena or a new adventure calls your name. When the transformation you are undergoing is more subtle in texture, like saying goodbye to an old habit, Moldavite will help you align with your new reality. Or try Shungite, Moss Agate or Tugtupite.

FORGIVENESS

Dioptase   Whether you need to be kinder to yourself or let go of hurt that someone else has caused you, forgiveness doesn't happen all at once. It's a process that you set in motion. Finding forgiveness requires self-love, self-worth and understanding. Dioptase can help you practice forgiveness by supporting you with its gentle and loving vibrations. You could also turn to Black Moonstone, Rhodochrosite or Pink Tourmaline.

WISDOM AND FREEDOM

Sagittarius season is represented by the archer who shoots high and blazes a trail into new territory. The archer is also a centaur – half horse and half human, half wild and half philosophical. Sagittarius season is a time to feel fiercely alive and simultaneously inspired to ask big, existential questions. It's a season for expanding your boundaries and traveling physically and mentally to understand more about the world and the human experience.

PISCES HOROSCOPE FOR SAGITTARIUS SEASON

The cosmic focus for Pisces is on work and career. Set your sights on new ambitions. Or, if you're already clear on your goals, discover ways to use your time more efficiently, or manage your resources with more practicality. You may find that you are busier than usual, so work smarter, not harder.

Morning Practice	Evening Practice
Go for a walk or a jog out in nature.	Memorize an inspiring quote.

CRYSTALS FOR SAGITTARIUS SEASON

INNER WISDOM

Azurite   In Sagittarius season, the archer knows that the best way to take aim is to trust your inner wisdom. When you are connected to your true self, it's easier to make choices. Life feels more satisfying. Azurite is the stone to hold and carry when you want to bolster your self-confidence and tune into your wisdom. Or choose Idocrase, Shattuckite or Amethyst.

EXPANSION

Jasper   Ruled by the gas giant Jupiter, Sagittarius is the sign of expansion. During this season, you can move beyond anything that is limiting you. Is there an area of your life in which you feel trapped in a cage? Maybe if you take a closer look, you'll find that the door to the cage has been open the entire time. Feel the freedom and expansion that is available to you with the help of Jasper. This enlivening stone will help you break out into new territory. Alternatives are Blue Topaz, Pink Chalcedony or Ruby Iolite.

ADVENTURE AND TRAVEL

Turquoise   When you're setting out in search of new horizons, reach for Turquoise as your talisman for protection and luck. Travel and adventure require equal parts bravery and boldness, but the reward is an expanded mindset and perspective. Let Turquoise be your steady support system as you push beyond your boundaries to discover excitement, new opportunity and enlightenment. You could also use Green Opal, Smoky Quartz or Aventurine.

CAREER AND GOALS

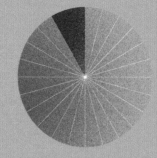

Like the mountain goat, in Capricorn season
you are primed to choose your footing carefully as
you make your ascent. Capricorn season brings practical
and productive forward motion. Use this energy efficiently
and tactically. You may choose to counterbalance this drive
and ambition with a large dose of acceptance, both
of yourself and others. Remember to give yourself a
break; you are trying your best.

PISCES HOROSCOPE FOR CAPRICORN SEASON

Enliven your mind with new hopes and dreams for the future! What is on your vision board? What inspires you? By asking yourself the right questions, you might find that you are flooded with brilliant ideas that can end up being quite life-changing. Find your inspiration by using your imagination and asking yourself deep questions.

Morning Practice

Write down your goals.

Evening Practice

Reflect on your
accomplishments.

CRYSTALS FOR
CAPRICORN SEASON

ACHIEVEMENT

Fluorite   Your Capricorn season recommendation supports
you in taking things one step at a time while staying focused
on your big picture goals. Look to Fluorite. Fluorite's unique
vibration can help you concentrate, while energizing you so
that you can keep moving forwards. Or look for support from
Ocean Jasper, Septarian Nodule or Tiger's Eye.

CAREER

Cat's Eye   Capricorn season is a wonderful time to take
stock. While you think about your work life, keep Cat's Eye by
your side. This stone helps you know your strengths, which is
imperative for a fulfilling career. It will help you feel optimistic
and believe in yourself. Cat's Eye's structured energy helps
you know your personal boundaries and make smart money
choices. You could also use Andradite Garnet, Apatite or
Hawk's Eye.

FOR SELF-ACCEPTANCE

Blue Aragonite   Let calming Blue Aragonite guide you
when you need to feel the soothing balm of self-acceptance.
Capricorn season pushes you to achieve, which may cause
you to question your progress in life. Counterbalance that by
learning to accept yourself for who you are. Blue Aragonite
has a compassionate energy that may inspire you to be less
judgemental towards yourself and show yourself more kindness.
Other crystals for self-acceptance are Prasiolite, Amethyst
or Shungite.

FRIENDSHIP
AND VISION

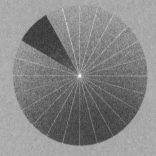

Aquarius season pushes people and ideas to the
forefront. What are your big ideas for the future?
And who is in your community? Your vision for the future
may also be a vision for humanity. Take the time to research
causes to which you might contribute time, money and
resources. Your friends, communities and social groups are
extra important during this season, so prioritize the people
who mean the most to you.

PISCES HOROSCOPE
FOR AQUARIUS SEASON

You may feel extra dreamy during
Aquarius season. The Sun is moving
through your area of dreams, the
subconscious, emotions and intuition.
Connect with yourself by taking a step
back from the demands of everyday life.
By slowing down, you'll tune into your
intuition and feel empowered to make
the choices that are right for you.

Affirmation
I LIVE IN THE MOMENT WITH HIGH HOPES FOR THE FUTURE.

Morning Practice	Evening Practice
Create a vision board and make it the first thing you see when you wake up.	Call a friend for a meaningful chat.

CRYSTALS FOR AQUARIUS SEASON

FRIENDSHIP

Bismuth   Aquarius season asks you to turn towards your community. What can you offer? What will you receive? Friends enrich your life in so many ways, but mostly by encouraging your feeling of belonging – a natural mood booster. Bismuth has an expansive energy that helps you join with others in a shared sense of community. Carry Bismuth as a reminder that you are connected to others. Or you could reach for Carnelian, Sunset Sodalite or Blue Apatite.

FAITH IN THE FUTURE

Cavansite   The future is uncertain. Sometimes you need a boost to help you trust in the potential and possibility of what the future can become. In that case, reach for Cavansite. This stone has a sweet vibe of positivity that can give you the courage to believe in your biggest dreams for the future. Some alternatives are Peridot, Muscovite or Auralite 23.

VIBRATIONAL LIFT

Apophyllite   When Aquarius season asks you to turn your attention to what is possible, it helps to have a positive outlook. Without suppressing any challenging feelings (those are important and need to be processed), pay some special attention to the positive things in your life and work to create an enduring, positive mindset. If you need a little extra support, reach for Clear or Green Apophyllite. This high-vibe crystal can lift your spirits and help you feel full of potential. You could also try Quartz, Hematite or Angelite.

71

INTUITION AND SPIRITUALITY

The most mystical season of all, Pisces season is the time to tune into your intuition. Slide like a slippery fish into the sphere of your dreams, faith, spirituality, compassion and creativity. This is a moment to rest, reflect and look inwards. Reconnect with your imagination. Feel your feelings. Plug into your spirituality or whatever makes you feel connected to the universe.

PISCES HOROSCOPE FOR PISCES SEASON

This is your special season! With the Sun moving through your sector of personality and identity, it's time to light up the room. People will notice you. Your energy is palpable, and you are radiant. What would be fun and exciting? This is a great time to feel free and spontaneous. Others are inspired when you express your unique spirit.

Morning Practice

Record your dreams.

Evening Practice

Do some freewriting
to clear your mind.

CRYSTALS FOR PISCES SEASON

COMPASSION

Lavender Quartz   Lavender Quartz helps you feel peace and understanding for others. It will bestow upon you the softness that you need to open up to other people's perspectives. It will also allow you to dissolve drama with a heightened sense of empathy. This soothing and healing stone can offer strength while you stand in someone else's shoes. A compassionate life is a fulfilling life. As an alternative, turn to Thulite, Prehnite with Epidote or Fluorite.

INTUITION

Pink Opal   When you trust your inner guidance system you have ultimate clarity. Harness the power of your intuition in Pisces season with the help of Pink Opal. This stone will help you connect to yourself and to your guides. It raises the volume on your inner 'Yes' or 'No' by quietening any distractions and helping you connect within. Other crystals for intuition are Clear Quartz, Moldavite or Dumortierite.

FOR FAITH

Celestite   Faith can be thought of as a complete trust or confidence in someone or something. With a little bit of faith you may find it easier to contend with fear or anxiety. But trust and faith must be developed from within. In Pisces season, harness the power of high-vibrational Celestite to help you move beyond unnecessary fears as you put your trust in something bigger. You could also use Vatican Stone, Apophyllite or Turquoise.

LUNAR ENERGY
AND MERCURY
IN MOTION

THE LUNAR CYCLE

In astrology, the Moon is a catalyst, helping us to move forwards with our goals and intentions.

The 29-day lunar cycle begins in darkness. The Moon then appears as a faint crescent and grows bigger until it's full. This process, from darkness to Full Moon, mirrors the incubation and development of your own creative process. Then, the Moon wanes until it completely disappears, reflecting another stage of the creative cycle – the process of releasing your efforts and making space for another cycle to begin. This allows new thoughts and ideas to emerge.

Each of the eight phases of the Moon cycle offers a different type of energy, which we will explore in this chapter. You can follow the Moon through the lunar month with crystal recommendations, setting your intentions in alignment with the New Moon and letting the lunar cycle help you make that intention into reality. The lunar cycle will also help you cleanse and release so that you can gently transition into the next phase.

By using crystals to work with the lunar cycle you can activate the potential of the Moon and amplify its energy. Through visualization or meditation, tap into the unique energies of each stage of the Moon cycle with the following crystals. For the suggested rituals at each phase, choose a crystal from the recommended options, or substitute with your favourite crystal.

Sun

New Moon

Waxing Crescent

Waning Crescent

First Quarter

Third Quarter

Earth

Waxing Gibbous

Waning Gibbous

Full Moon

SET YOUR NEW INTENTIONS

The Moon is dark. This is a time for reflection and a time to connect with your inner self. Use your energy to envision what you would like to make happen. What do you desire? What are your dreams? Anything is possible – imagine that you are planting seeds of intention that will manifest and grow throughout the Waxing Moon Phase. The New Moon is a quiet and emotional time and you may discover that, as you think about what you would like to create, many different feelings arise. Excitement, anticipation, fear, worry – whatever feelings arise, make space for those feelings and be gentle with yourself. Listen to your intuition and imagine your next steps.

Black Moonstone can support you during the delicate and sensitive New Moon vibration. It offers wellsprings of patience and peace as you work with your emotions and reflect on your life. When your dreams are germinating under the surface, Black Moonstone can help you trust your own process.

Labradorite opens your third eye wide so that you can tune into your intuition, and design your goals in accordance with your path and purpose.

Pink Sapphire's loving energy can buffer you and help you feel emotionally at ease.

Ametrine provides sweet joy and concentrated focus so that you can set intentions with confidence.

TRUST,
INSPIRATION, SERENITY
AND DELIGHT

New Moon Ritual

Freewrite about what you yearn for and anything else that's on your mind. Then jot down your intentions for this Moon cycle on a piece of paper and place your chosen crystal on top.

NURTURE YOUR INTENTIONS

Your seeds of intention are germinating under the soil, and maybe some of the plants are just beginning to sprout. As the lunar energy builds momentum, make sure that you have the resources you need to achieve your goals. Provide structure and support for yourself. This cycle is just beginning to take shape, so consider how your choices will determine your direction – maybe there are changes you'd like to make to your goals. Remain curious throughout this process, because anything is possible!

Turquoise is a powerhouse of a crystal that can deftly carry you through the precarious Waxing Crescent phase. At this moment you need a subtle combination of confidence, discernment, curiosity and commitment. Turquoise can help you understand the truth of what you need to create, and it can help you stay open and accepting of your process. Use this stone as you decide what you really want to manifest and commit to during this Moon cycle.

Shattuckite helps you intuitively illuminate your path so that you can make the decisions that are right for you.

Pyrite offers crystalline protection and is a wonderful choice to help you realize your goals.

Orange Calcite gives you mental focus and lots of energy for the journey ahead.

TRUTH, INTUITION, MANIFESTATION AND FOCUS

Waxing Crescent Moon Ritual

Read and rewrite your intentions for this Moon cycle.
Decorate the paper and place your chosen crystal back on top.

BUILD YOUR MOMENTUM

Look around your garden of intentions and discover what is growing. Have your goals started to take shape? If so, how are they coming along? Do you need more support? Perhaps you have had surprising results? At the First Quarter Moon the constraints of reality can be intimidating. You have big dreams, but sometimes you encounter resistance when dreams make contact with real world limitations. Maybe there is more work required than you had foreseen, or there are real-world issues with time, money, support or other resources. Give yourself lots of encouragement. Pivot, and reassess if necessary. This is an exciting, high energy time, so keep taking action and building momentum.

Bumblebee Jasper When reality, and all of its limitations, hits, Bumblebee Jasper can help you stay the course with confidence. Lean on this crystal when you need the energy to just keep moving forwards. It will subdue your fears and inspire you to push past your comfort zone.

Peridot is a cheery companion that will help you look at any situation with optimism.

Tangerine Quartz offers creative potential that makes problem solving effortless.

Aventurine will vitalize you and give you the confidence to keep going.

CONFIDENCE,
OPTIMISM, CREATIVITY AND
VITALITY

First Quarter Moon Ritual

Light a candle, hold your chosen crystal and visualize your intentions being realized.

DEVELOP YOUR INTENTIONS

It's astonishing what a little effort can create! Now that you've made it to the Waxing Gibbous phase of the Moon cycle, you are starting to see the effects of the intentions that you set. If your goal was to improve your nutrition, you may be feeling better already. If you felt motivated to get out there and start dating, you may have started some new conversations. Whatever the last few days have revealed, now is the time to roll up your sleeves and actively give shape to your garden. What will you weed out? What is working, and what isn't working? What changes might you make? The intensity has almost peaked so take tender care of your emotional well-being as you keep putting in effort towards your dreams.

Jet Jet's grounding energy will help you establish deep root systems for your developing intentions. When you need strength and motivation to keep pushing forwards with your goals, this stone will support you. As a bonus, jet has a sheltering vibration that can steady you emotionally and help you surge forwards with optimism and hope.

Hematite offers balance and protection, helping you proactively take care of yourself during this active time.

Carnelian lights your fire with sparkling enthusiasm and convinces you to tune into your creative side.

Blue Lace Agate calms your mind, allowing you to weed through your options and make solid decisions.

GROUNDING,
PROTECTION, ENTHUSIASM
AND PEACE OF MIND

Waxing Gibbous Moon Ritual

While holding or wearing your chosen crystal, do something that feels active or expressive, such as dancing, painting, gardening, cooking or singing. Imagine your goals and repeat your intentions.

HARVEST

Everything is revealed under the light of the Moon. The attempts you've made, your wins, your losses. It's time to get out in the garden and harvest the crop. Regardless of whether the bounty lives up to your expectations, there is something to appreciate and celebrate. At the Full Moon, honour what you've created and give gratitude to yourself for your commitment. This phase represents the push and pull of two opposite energies as the Moon is in the opposite sign to the Sun. The result is a highly polarized and intense energy that can heighten emotions, pull you in two different directions, or cause you to realize something important. Make sure to be very gentle with yourself and those around you.

EMOTIONAL EXPLORATION, ABUNDANCE, PEACEFULNESS AND RECEPTIVITY

White Moonstone symbolizes the Full Moon and all of its glorious creativity and excitement. This pearly white crystal shines a bright light so that you can see clearly. As you examine the fruits that you've cultivated during the Waxing Moon phase, use the receptive and healing energy of White Moonstone to help you accept and celebrate. It's time for gratitude, and this comforting crystal will help you open up to that feeling.

Green Apatite is an antidote to the drama of the Full Moon – use it to highlight joy and abundance.

Jade has a subtle, soothing energy that imparts an optimistic attitude.

Stilbite connects the heart, mind and intuition – this can help you rationally balance your emotions while still opening up to divine insight.

Full Moon Ritual

Hold your chosen crystal and write down three things that you are grateful for. The Full Moon is also a great time to cleanse your crystals. Place them outside or on a windowsill and let them bathe in the Moon's healing energy.

REFLECT AND REVIEW

Now that the intensity of the full reveal has begun to wane, you can settle deeper into your new reality. Indulge yourself and enjoy. As the Moon has moved through waxing to waning, this is the beginning of a less active and more receptive phase. This means that you can simply sit with the ebbing fullness of what is. Begin a process of compassionate review. What have you learned? What will you do differently in the next Moon cycle? Each lunar cycle reveals an older, more experienced version of who you are becoming. So sink into this moment of reflection and get to know yourself once more.

Obsidian offers a protective energy that buffers and supports. Use it at the Waning Gibbous phase of the Moon cycle to release the past and securely recline into the experience of the moment. Obsidian's cleansing vibes can help you remove any junk from your thought patterns, allowing you to think from a new perspective. Harness its clarifying energy to appraise your situation with equanimity and objectivity.

Tiger's Eye is for encouragement and strength as you review your progress and make plans for improvement.

Citrine offers joy and optimism so that you can look at your accomplishments through a positive lens.

Celestite provides tranquillity as you come down off the high of the Full Moon.

PROTECTION,
STRENGTH, JOY AND
TRANQUILLITY

Waning Gibbous Moon Ritual

Pour yourself some tea, water, or other drink of your choice, and take the time to sit and quietly appreciate the moment. With your chosen crystal nearby, review your intention and gratitude lists.

LET GO

Get comfortable letting go so that you can make space for new things. At the Last Quarter Moon allow the leaves to fall and the fading plants to return to the soil. A tree drops its leaves to conserve resources. Take stock of what you want to let go of, so that you can use your energy wisely. Is there someone you need to forgive? Do you need to release your expectations and accept something about your life? Release the past or an outdated way of thinking, let go and forgive. Maybe you declutter your closet, acknowledge your reality, admit your mistakes, get really honest with yourself, or forgive yourself or others. The Last Quarter Moon asks that you put in a little effort to let go of the emotions and ideas that are taking up excess energy.

Rose Quartz is an emotional balm that can help you forgive yourself and others. As the Last Quarter Moon inspires you to release your expectations and accept your current reality, you need a soothing support that helps you open up compassionately. Rose Quartz brings playful, loving vibes and helps you gently accept a situation and move forwards.

Rutilated Quartz offers a powerful support in following through on your intentions as you review what you've learned and plan for the next phase.

Smoky Quartz provides grounding, protection and assistance in clearing the thoughts and feelings that you are ready to release.

Amethyst is for gently releasing old mental patterns and contemplating new possibilities.

LOVE, SUPPORT, GROUNDING AND GENTLE SELF-REFLECTION

Last Quarter Moon Ritual

Create a peaceful environment and run a bath for yourself. Place a water-safe, non-toxic crystal (such as Quartz or Amethyst) in the bath while you review your intentions from this moon cycle. Repeat these affirmations, 'I make space for clarity' and 'I release the past'.

STILLNESS AND REST

The lunar energy is encouraging you to turn inwards and be still. All is quiet in the winter of your metaphorical garden. Embracing stillness offers many benefits. By allowing your inner landscape to exist without judgement, you honour who you are now. Slowing down can also help you uncover your values and emotional truth – which may not be so apparent when you are busily running around. And last but not least, rest and quiet will help you recharge your energy for the next cycle. Challenge yourself to slow down and be present in the moment. There will be ample time for new plans and dreams when the next cycle begins.

Serpentine can help you open a gateway to the stillness within and to the profound interconnectedness of the universe. Using this crystal during your Waning Crescent Moon meditations will help you feel buffered and supported in the understanding that there is no-one you need to be and nothing you need to do. Float along with the waves of existence. You'll know when the time is right again for action.

Selenite radiates cleansing energy that can help you release the past cycle and prepare to make a fresh start.

Howlite soothes your spirit and quietens any absurd complaints from your 'inner critic'.

Aquamarine helps you create a meditative state of mind so that you can listen to the stillness within.

CONNECTION WITH NATURE, CLEANSING, SOOTHING AND REFLECTION

Waning Crescent Moon Ritual

Sit quietly in the meditation of your choosing. Hold your crystal or place it nearby.

MERCURY
RETROGRADE

Mercury Retrograde deserves attention as it's a chance to review your plans and goals. It's notoriously known for causing technology and communication issues, but the upside of this time period is that it offers an invitation to slow down and re-assess where you are and where you want to go.

Fast-moving Mercury symbolizes connection, communication and technology. Mercury is the part of you that learns, thinks, teaches and talks.

Mercury orbits the Sun about four times as fast as the Earth and every time that Mercury zips past the Earth an optical illusion occurs that makes it look as though Mercury is moving backwards. When Mercury appears to be moving backwards (Mercury Retrograde), it's a great opportunity to slow down. Go back over your thoughts and decisions of recent months and review them. Turn inwards to gain guidance from your intuition.

Mercury Retrograde happens about three times a year and lasts for about three weeks each time. You can use these retrograde periods as a moment to check in with yourself and review your practices, thoughts and relationships. Have you been putting off an uncomfortable conversation? Is there something that you need to be honest about with yourself when it comes to relationships, work or money? What has your body been trying to tell you? Is there some new way that you could step out of your comfort zone? What would help you feel more secure and supported?

Underlying issues tend to rise to the surface during Mercury Retrograde. It's typically advised to make sure that you are extra clear in your communications during these periods, and that you wait until the retrograde period has ended before beginning new projects or signing contracts. But it's an excellent time to pick up where you left off on something – to rethink, redo and review.

YOUR CRYSTAL PRACTICE DURING MERCURY RETROGRADE

Crystal energy can help you slow down your busy mind and tune into your intuition during Mercury Retrograde. As you rethink and review, these crystals will amplify your intuition and clarity.

KEEN INSIGHT

Pietersite   Employ this speckled Quartz for illuminated insight paired with steady determination.

CLARITY AND COMMUNICATION

Aquamarine   This stone soothes and calms the mind while simultaneously boosting your ability to communicate clearly.

CREATIVE THOUGHT

Citrine   A crystal that spurs your imagination, helping you conceptualize how you might like patterns or situations to change.

Beginning of Mercury Retrograde Ritual	End of Mercury Retrograde Ritual
Perform a full and gentle review of the issues most affecting you by writing a journal entry using the following prompt: 'What do I need to see that I'm not seeing when it comes to my …' Give yourself lots of gratitude in the process and call on your chosen crystal to provide understanding and clarity. When you've finished, write down three takeaways on a small piece of paper and place your crystal on top of it for the remainder of the Retrograde. Drawing on the power of your crystal, let your subconscious mind continue to explore and reveal the subtleties of these thoughts and questions over the coming weeks.	Near the end of the Retrograde cycle, set an intention to integrate what you've learned during the past days and weeks. Begin by returning to your piece of paper and your crystal. What came up for you during Mercury Retrograde? Was there a new realization, attitude or interest that emerged? Think about what you may have realized and journal about what you'd like to bring into your life now. Is there an intention (see page 22) or affirmation that could come from this exploration? If so, write it down. Look in a mirror and repeat your intention or affirmation five times while holding your crystal. Remember to thank your crystal and to thank yourself for showing up. For the next two weeks, repeat this daily ritual.

CONCLUSION

This book has taken you deep below the Earth's surface, through the metaphorical caverns of crystals and their symbolism. You've connected the dots of the solar system and the meaning of the astrology you were born with. By pairing the forces of the stars above with the crystals below, you've gained tools that can help you navigate your unique journey with wisdom.

In Part Two, you learned about the crystals that can support your unique astrology. This section included insights for Pisces Sun, Moon and Rising signs, along with supportive crystal recommendations for what your sign needs in five key life areas.

Life is always changing and so in Part Three you learned to follow the energy of the Sun as it moves on its annual journey through the zodiac, finding crystals that may help

you elaborate on the theme of each astrological season.

Revolving and evolving with changing astrological cycles continued in Part Four, where you paired crystal energy with the ebb and flow of the Moon, and learned to harness the power of crystals in tandem with Mercury Retrograde to perform a trimonthly check-in.

All the answers are already within you. When you choose a crystal, you awaken the vibration of that crystal within yourself. Harness your astro-crystal practice to help you see what already exists inside of you. You have everything you need.

With the cosmos above and the crystals below, you are always connected and supported. Let the stones and the stars strengthen your self-awareness and self-trust as you continue your crystalline cosmic journey.

Crystals and astrology are not intended to be a substitute for medical advice, diagnosis or treatment. Always seek the advice of your qualified healthcare provider.

RESORCES

GET YOUR BIRTH CHART	www.sandysitron.com/crystals
ASTROLOGY READING	www.sandysitron.com
CRYSTALS	***101 Power Crystals:*** *The Ultimate Guide to Magical Crystals, Gems, and Stones for Healing and Transformation* Judy Hall
CRYSTAL ENERGY HEALING	https://www.kalisaaugustine.com/
SOURCING CRYSTALS RESPONSIBLY	moonrisecrystals.com/
SPIRAL CRYSTALS	spiralcrystals.com/
HOOF AND PAW	hoofandpawuk.com/
ASTROLOGY	***Astrology for Yourself*** Demetra George and Douglas Bloch
AFFIRMATION WORK	Transformational coach Dana Balicki: https://danabalicki.com/
AFFIRMATION WORK	***Empowerment:*** *The Art of Creating Your Life as You Want It* Gail Straub and David Gershon
ASTROLOGY EDUCATION	www.thestrology.com
	Ritual Enchantments *A Modern Witch's Guide to Self-Possession* Mya Spalter

FEATURED CRYSTALS